MICHAEL J. STABILE, Ph.D

Remember the
BAMBOO?
Cultivating a
GROWTH
CULTURE

Empowering Papa's Legacy

outskirts
press

Remember the Bamboo? Cultivating a Growth Culture
Empowering Papa's Legacy
All Rights Reserved.
Copyright © 2023 Michael J. Stabile, Ph.D.
v4.0

The opinions expressed in this manuscript are solely the opinions of the author and do not represent the opinions or thoughts of the publisher. The author has represented and warranted full ownership and/or legal right to publish all the materials in this book.

This book may not be reproduced, transmitted, or stored in whole or in part by any means, including graphic, electronic, or mechanical without the express written consent of the publisher except in the case of brief quotations embodied in critical articles and reviews.

Outskirts Press, Inc.
http://www.outskirtspress.com

ISBN: 978-1-9772-6205-9

Cover Photo © 2023 www.gettyimages.com. All rights reserved - used with permission.

Outskirts Press and the "OP" logo are trademarks belonging to Outskirts Press, Inc.

PRINTED IN THE UNITED STATES OF AMERICA

Dedication

This book's beginnings can be traced to a coffee shop over coffee with a friend. Those conversations led us on a journey to put the "Bamboo Principles" into practical application with my friend's team and organization. While the characters, events, and story are fictional they evolved from those original conversations and work we partnered in. Thank you Frank Riley for your trust, belief, and willingness to step out in faith to apply the principles contained in this book.

Table of Contents

The Prologue i
1. The Crisis Crossroad 1
2. They Just Don't Get It... 4
3. Defining a Winning Culture..................................... 9
4. The Feedback 13
5. The Bamboo Story 17
6. Remove the Hindrances to Growth 24
7. The Process is Slow and Fast................................. 28
8. A Strong and Deep Root System 33
9. Believe and Commit to the Process 36
10. The Leadership Mindset 41
11. The Process of Developing a Healthy Culture 49
12. The Bamboo is Growing 56
Epilogue 62
References 64
About The Author 69

Acknowledgments

WHY THIS BOOK?

The foundations of this story have been the foundations of my life's work in *transforming cultures one person at a time*.

I love to tell a good story a "sticky" story one that is full of principles, deeper meaning, and practical applications. The Bamboo Story is that kind of story. I'd like to acknowledge a few of the people and relationships that have influenced the story you are now reading.

My former students at Xavier University (Cincinnati, OH), my past and present clients, and most of all my family. To my lovely bride, Pam, our daughters Sara, Jessica, and Christina, son-in-loves Joe, Brian, and Tommie, and our grandchildren, Jonas, Nolan, Lucy, Sophia, Evie, Penny, and Luca. A special thank you to our team at FutureNow Consulting: Pam, Christina, and Sara. What you do, how you do it, and how you serve our clients gives me the opportunity, motivation, and passion to pursue writing books like this.

To Christina Shimrock, thank you again for your editorial skills and work on the initial manuscript and drafts. Your ability, talent, and advice have been greatly appreciated.

Thank you to the editorial team at Outskirts Press. Your professional services and customer service are outstanding, and I know you have made this book better as a result.

The legendary organizational and leadership guru Peter Drucker put the essence of culture in the following language: *"Culture Eats Strategy for Breakfast."* Culture is essentially the *organizational air* we breathe. Like air, culture is often not seen directly. Rather, it is seen indirectly through how organizational members engage in their work, how they behave, how they embody group norms, and how they live out espoused values.

Other authors, such as Patrick Lencioni in *The Advantage*, highlight the vital dimension of culture. He argues that organizational health is the greatest opportunity for organizational improvement and competitive advantage. In contrast to what he refers to as **smart** business—engaging fundamentals like strategy, marketing, finance, and technology—organizational **health** is the real place where competitive advantage may shine beyond the first half of the equation of smart business.

Think of it as the collection of traits that make your company what it is. A great culture exemplifies positive traits that lead to improved performance, while a dysfunctional company culture brings out qualities that can hinder even the most successful organizations. Don't confuse culture with organizational goals or a mission statement, although both can help define it. Culture is created through consistent and authentic behaviors, not press releases or policy documents. You can watch company culture in action when you see how a leader responds to a crisis, how a team adapts to new customer demands, or how a manager corrects an employee who makes a mistake.

This book is the third in the Papa's Legacy Leadership

Parable series. Follow the journey of James (Jim) Thor, an up and coming CEO of a small but growing family-owned real estate and facilities management business and his interactions with his executive leadership coach Dr. Jonas Nolan. He has dreamed of the day when they would take a bigger stage and customer to be in the top tier of their industry, and that day had arrived! However, after the first few euphoric weeks of working with their new customer, the company began to experience a series of ongoing disappointments. Jim was feeling the enormous pressure of this mammoth change that in his mind was overwhelming. Someone had to be accountable for the mess, and Jim was the person at the top. He was now facing his deepest fear—failure. *"How can leadership be this hard?"*

Join Jim in his conversations and encounters with Dr. Jonas Nolan as he shares the principles of building a healthy and winning culture through the lessons he learned from his Papa: "The Bamboo Story Principles".

The Prologue

"This is an opportunity of a life time, but no one seems to care. I just don't understand why they aren't getting it!" Jim continued to amp up his workout on the elliptical as these thoughts overwhelmed him.

His own inner voice taunted him as he continued his inner dialogue. *Maybe I don't have enough experience to pull this off. There are so many new people, new territories, and almost unrealistic customer demands. I don't know if I'm 'good enough' to work through all of those challenges.*

Just three months ago, Jim and his organization were excited that they won the contract with one of the fastest growing and expanding banks in the Midwest. They now had a presence in over 25 states and projected to expand to all 50 states over the next 5-10 years.

He recalls the day he was asked to be the CEO of a small but growing family owned real estate and facilities management business. Although he was not a family member, he had been treated like family and knew that the family believed he was the right choice to expand and move them forward. Together they worked on a seemly indestructible business plan and a proven track record for success locally. They dreamed of this day when they would take a bigger stage to be in the top tier of their industry. However, after the first few euphoric weeks of working with their new customer, the company began to experience a series of ongoing disappointments.

Critical deadlines started to slip. A few key employees below the executive level unexpectedly left the company. Morale deteriorated gradually as this once very tight knit family business began going through the growing pains of adjusting to the larger corporate environment. They were almost forced by the customer and contract to hire former bank employees that would now be absorbed into their business and culture. Jim was feeling the enormous pressure of this mammoth change and he was experiencing the effects of being overworked, overcommitted, and overwhelmed.

The bank was growing impatient with the stumbling of Jim and his team. They were losing faith that they had made the right decision in going with this smaller ambitious company. There was just too much at stake for the future of the bank and its long range plans to be more understanding with the transition and change process.

Someone had to be accountable for the mess, and Jim was the person at the top. He was now facing his deepest fear — failure. How can leadership be this hard? Over the last several years he had been on the fast track to success or at least what he thought success should be. When he became the CEO of the company, they encouraged him about the importance of a mentor and leadership coach. He was reluctant, but he followed through and met with the coach. Jim kept the coach's advice at arms length and just went through the motions. He did see some very helpful skills and habits start to manifest both personally and professionally. However, now he felt vulnerable, exposed, and ashamed. He had never really failed before, at least not like this. All eyes were on him and his team. He thought to himself. *Could it be my deepest fear is now being exposed and being brought to light? What will I do next?* Jim knew he needed to act and deal with thes be deep-seated fears and emotions that were controlling and haunting him. He needed help and he needed it fast.

He quickly powered down the elliptical machine and toweled off the beading sweat from his brow and face. Pulling out his cell phone, he thumbed through his contacts and found the number. "Hello, Jonas. Could you meet with me ASAP? I have to talk to you, it is URGENT!"

1.

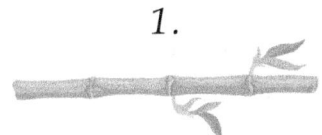

The Crisis Crossroad

Dr. Jonas Nolan was caught off guard by the sudden and unexpected phone call from James Thor. As he listened to Jim's urgency to meet, he knew that something was going on that finally was getting through to him. Jonas was Jim's executive leadership coach, but he hadn't heard from him in over a month. In fact, he had tried to make several contacts either through email, text, and phone, but either Jim would not get back to him or he had an urgent meeting that would not allow them to connect.

He couldn't help but smile as he listened to the message Jim left on his phone. Over the past year, Jim was going through the motions of the leadership coaching process. He had an answer for everything and always a legitimate excuse, at least in his mind, for why he was not following through. Jonas had learned over the years that patience was the key in coaching high-performers, especially those at this point in their role and careers. He knew by personal experience how high-performers who are in the fast track in their professions could easily develop blind spots, pride, and selfishness.

Jonas knew that Jim was under tremendous stress and pressure with the new customer and the change process. In fact, he had tried to get Jim to work within on preparing for the process of culture change that would shock his organization. But in Jim's typical way of handling pressures, he assured Jonas that he was confident that he had this and had prepared himself and his company for this drastic change process. In reality, he couldn't know what he didn't know because he was too busy celebrating the contract win and was caught-up with his and the company's past experience and track record. He had a major blind spot. However, over the years, Jonas' personal experience in leading major change transitions as well as working with multiple clients through similar situations, he knew Jim was exhibiting a very familiar pattern that he had seen too many times before.

Jonas reflected back to his own life and crisis that lead him to break down the walls of self-preservation that blinded and hindered him. The journey of 1,000 miles always begins with the first step. His first step, at the time, was a huge leap. He came to a crossroads of conscience and heart belief.

He remembered the advice of Papa, his grandfather. "The way back home always begins with humility. Just like the parable of the Prodigal Son, selfish pride keeps us from realizing who and what we really are. *Humility is the ability to be you.* A decision today to affect the future begins when we get a glimpse of our 'true self' and then choose. You have to evaluate your past and your potential and step toward one or the other."

Over twenty-five years ago, he stood at the podium to give the biggest talk, on the biggest stage of his career. He was the keynote speaker to the annual meeting of the International Council on Leadership. It was a climactic day for Jonas and his family. His lifelong body of work, research, and teaching had brought him to this pinnacle event. Over the years, a who's who of the most inspirational, motivational, and influential experts on leadership had been asked to give the keynote address to this prestigious group of international leaders. Jonas was conflicted. In that moment, he had experienced a series of paradoxical thoughts that all began with 'if' and ended with 'then'.

Jonas remembered vividly how he took a deep breath and began his speech, "For too many years, I have spent my life focused on me. I realized that it is time for my heart to catch up with my head. I am a selfish, prideful man. The only person I have really ever served has been myself. I wanted to be great, but tonight it is very clear with all my accomplishments, I have built my house upon the sand. I made the study of leadership my life and I tell you all here in this auditorium: that is not real leadership! I, like many of you, have a leader-first mentality. It has been motivated by power, position, material possessions, and prestige. With all of my so-called accomplishments and activities there really has been very little transformational change in the people my life has intersected. Tonight, all of that is going to change!"

Jonas said out loud this time, "The journey of 1,000 miles always begins with the first step. My first step, at the time, was a huge leap. I came to a crossroads of conscience and heart belief."

Jonas reflected on the words he heard from John Maxwell, author and leadership expert, in a podcast. Maxwell shared a definition about a decision that is a turning point.

"When it comes to a crisis: The dictionary defines crisis as "an intense time of great difficulty. The medical term crisis means "a turning point. In Greek, crisis means decision." And his definition combines all three: "A time of intense difficulty, requiring a decision, that is a turning point."

Was Jim at the point of crisis, of intense difficulty requiring a decision that will lead to a turning point in his life?

2.

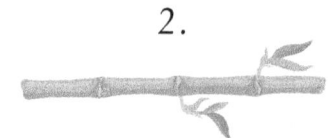

They Just Don't Get It

On the drive to the Back Street Café to meet Jonas Nolan, Jim had been struggling with his current situation. He was driven by ambition, or so he thought. He wanted to be on the fast track, but to his chagrin he felt derailed. Here he was a CEO with a major contract with a growing and major client, but he was failing He had never really failed before, at least not like this. The magnitude, the embarrassment, the humiliation was too much for him to even contemplate.

"Jim, we need you to get hold of this situation or we will find someone else who can," the voice of, Cheryl Chatwood, CEO of the bank word's still ignited emotion as he felt his face reddening. Cheryl was a high profile executive and was growing impatient with Jim and his team. As much as he protested and argued that everything was fine and that he and his team would be able to handle it, he couldn't help but feel hopeless and helpless. "Jim, you need help and you need it now!" And with those words still ringing in his ears, he turned into the parking lot at the Back Street Café.

"How did I get to this point in my life?" The last thing he consciously remembered about the drive was getting into the car and then he was driving on autopilot.

Jim was a self-starter, a go-getter, focused on reputation,

status, opportunity, and most of all he wanted to be successful in everything he did. From the time he was very young, his father drilled into his thinking, "Jimmy, work harder than everybody, walk with pride, do whatever you have to succeed. And Jimmy, never–never embarrass me or our family."

He was now at a place he never thought he would be in his life and career. He didn't have an answer; he really didn't know what to do next. He was stuck, stressed, and stumbling!

Jim distractedly walked through the doors and didn't notice that an elderly lady with a cane was trying to open the door and holding tightly to her coffee cup. He was so deep in thought and focused on his own problems, he failed to notice someone that needed a helping hand as he headed to the host stand. Jonas had been watching for Jim from his booth near the entrance, but now his focus was on the elderly lady. He leaped to his feet and opened the door for her. "Would you like me to help you to your car?" She nodded her head and Jonas grabbed the coffee from her so that it wouldn't spill and walked her to the car.

Jim looked around and wondered where Jonas was off to. Gus, the owner of the café' pointed to Jonas helping the women to her car and brought a fresh cup of coffee to the booth where Jonas had been sitting. "He'll be right back", and gestured for Jim to sit down in Jonas' booth. "You know Jonas, he is always ready to serve."

"Jim, my friend, how are you doing?" Jonas said with a smile and a twinkle in his eyes as he hurriedly came back into the cafe and immediately shook Jim's hand.

"How are Penny and the kids? Jonas said with genuine care. Jim knew Dr. Jonas Nolan cared deeply about him. He had demonstrated that repeatedly to him over the past year. He also knew that he could trust him. There had been some really vulnerable moments in their coaching interactions, but he always handled them with the utmost integrity. But most of all deep in his heart he knew Jonas could help him. In fact, he may be the only person he knew who could help him to work through this mess he was now facing.

Jim reluctantly and cautiously filled Jonas in on Penny and the kids, but in his heart he knew that he had really been an absentee husband and father. That is one of the reasons with all of his busyness he didn't get back to Jonas. He knew deep down that he wasn't making them a priority. Dr. Nolan had a way of seeing right through him and he felt the shame of his own neglect. It was him, it was really his own conscious, but right now he couldn't focus on anything but making sure he didn't lose this bank customer. As he was deep in his own thoughts, his inner self-talk keeps disrupting him. *Yes, family is important, but if you can't provide for them, if you get fired, you've failed, they can't be proud of you, and worst of all you are a failure.*

"You look like you are a million miles away," Jonas' words brought him back into the conversation. "Why don't you tell me why you called me with the urgency to meet this morning?"

"They just don't get it," Jim abruptly blurted out with fierce emotion.

"Tell me more, what do you mean they just don't get it? First who doesn't get and what do they need to get?"

Jim adjusted his glasses and leaned into the table and began. "My team, specifically the new expanded team, with members that in many instances were forced on us by our new customer, the bank. As you know, after we landed this big deal, we had to expand rapidly and the bank wanted us to assimilate many of their employees and accommodate them.

Of course, they had to go through the interview and rehiring process, but you know how that goes, there is always pressure to take people who you would have never considered otherwise."

After a pause to reflect on what he just heard, he took a sip of his coffee before it got cold. He was following Jim's train of thought, but he wanted to clarify even further, "So what is it that your new expanded team doesn't get?"

"They don't get our culture, they just don't fit! They are resistant and not willing to change and work together like a team. We have always prided ourselves on having team players. As a whole, we have people who feel like they need special treatment and are acting like superstars who are too good for us. They just don't treat people right, they don't want to go the extra mile that is needed to be successful."

"Let me see if I understand, you have the plan, processes, systems, in place; however, they were not getting the behavior and/or attitude to support the plan, processes, and systems. So the real question is: How do we cultivate a growing culture and maintain our heart values of service and humility across expanding and diverse demographics?"

Jim smiled and nodded, "Yes, that's exactly right and I know it when I see it, and to date, I'm not seeing it."

Jonas repeated back to Jim, "So you know it when you see it!" But how does your team know what 'IT' is?"

Jim looked like a deer in highlights. "I . . .um, I guess they really should know how to treat people and how the customer should be at the center of everything we do. But isn't that just common sense?"

"Yes and no," Jonas quickly added. "Are your values clearly articulated so that everyone is clear about what 'IT' is?"

"If you are asking if I have a mission statement and a strategic plan then the answer is absolutely yes!"

Jonas sat up in the booth and leaned in and looked Jim right in the eyes, "No, I'm asking about your culture, your values, how you want people to behave, respond, and the attitude that goes with those values and beliefs. Mission is WHERE you are going. Strategy is HOW you are going to get there. But culture is WHY and WHO you are."

"Well, I guess the answer to your question is no. We don't have a clearly defined and articulated culture. I just assumed people would get 'IT' when they joined us." Jim looked down at his coffee cup before he took the next sip.

"So let me get this straight. You are upset and frustrated with your team because they are not getting the culture, but there is nothing that clarifies what it is and it is not explicitly being taught. You are expanding your team exponentially and demographically and they are failing to live up to your culture and your values of doing business."

Jim held his coffee cup to his mouth but it was like he was frozen in time with Jonas' words. He thought to himself, *but come on, Jonas; this is just basic common sense everyone should get it, right!*

Jonas waited for his words to sink in and then said, "So here is what I just heard, your team should read your mind and know exactly what are your company values and then behave accordingly."

At that point it hit Jim. "The real problem here is me as a leader, I haven't clearly articulated WHO we are and WHY we value what we value and believe."

3.

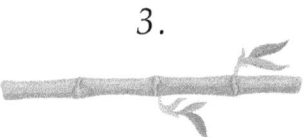

Defining a Winning Culture

Jonas knew he had Jim's undivided attention probably for the first time since their coaching relationship began. He was starting to see that leadership couldn't start with mission, strategy, or methodology. It must start with PEOPLE. The collective attitude, belief, and behavior of people make-up the culture. Culture is the WHO we are and WHY we exist. As Simon Sinek, author and speaker, so famously coined, "Start with WHY." The health of any organization lies in the core values and beliefs that are the roots and foundation that clearly identify and represent how people are to think and behave.

"Jim, leaders are very clear about their values, and about the difference between right or wrong. They knew what they stand for and what they will not stand for. Remember, everything does rise and fall on leadership. It is what you are creating and what you are allowing. Frankly, if you are honest with yourself, the problem isn't with your team. The problem is YOU!"

Jim's eyes dropped and he put his coffee cup down on the table and started to slouch in the booth. There was an awkward silence as Jim digested Jonas' words, "The problem is YOU!"

Internally, he was getting angry, not with Jonas and his

words, but at himself, he knew Jonas was right. He was not leading, he had become the victim and he was blaming his team and the circumstances and not taking ownership for his lack of leadership.

"You're right, I am the problem and I've been looking for someone or something to put the blame on for my failure. I created this and I'm the one responsible for the culture, especially holding people up to the beliefs and values of our company."

"So let's begin by defining your culture. *What does a winning culture value and believe?*" Jonas could see the fire return to Jim's eyes, but there was something different this time. He had a humble and teachable spirit that was not just driven by his own personal ambition. Jim's pride began to break down and he was now ready to be the leader he was meant to be.

"Let's start with getting clear on what you value and believe and put that down on paper. Your company has had a great reputation for many years long before you became the CEO. So tell me what makes your organization great?" Jonas reached down for his notebook and tore out a piece of paper for Jim and himself to take notes.

Jim took sometime time to think and reflect and he started to jot down some values and beliefs that were the heart of his company. "The very first thing that I wrote down was safety. We always have made safety not only a value, but that we also care about all of our associates and customers. Their safety is first and foremost in our thinking each and every day. In fact, we have built safety as one of our key performance indicators in all of our contracts. Further, aligned with safety is our customer focus. We believe the customer must be the center of everything we do. I believe that is why we have been so successful in the past."

Jonas was feeling the energy that Jim was now exhibiting. He was getting down to the roots of what the company valued, believed, and who they are. He was focusing on the core values and beliefs that made the organization and him successful.

About 45 minutes into the exercise of brainstorming and clarifying the core beliefs and values, they had synthesized the list down to seven core values. Jonas looked directly into Jim's eyes, "If you asked your team and/or customers, would they identify these values and beliefs about your company?"

Jim adjusted his glasses and looked over the list and pondered the question through the grid of those core values. "I hope so! However, as for me, yes, these seven core values fully represent what I meant when I said they do get it. These values are the IT! However, I really do understand now that they have never clearly been articulated, written, or used as part of the hiring or training process."

It was like a light switch has just been turned on for Jim. For the first time since they started this new contract with the bank he felt hopeful that they could succeed.

"So now that we have these core values, what do I do next?" Jim realized that he still didn't know how to communicate or take the next steps to begin the process of cultivating his business culture.

Jonas quickly responded, "Two things. First, we need to create an easy way to memorize the values by using an acronym or mantra that consolidates these values. Second, you need to test them and ask for feedback from your team and customers to see if they resonate as to WHO you are and WHY you exist as a company."

They spent the next 30 minutes working on an easy way to remember the values. Suddenly, Jim smiled and with the excitement of someone who just hit his first homerun said, "I've got it! You know what you always say, 'To serve is to lead!' How about S.E.R.V.I.C.E.?"

Jim took time to write down the letters of **SERVICE** on the page and turned it around so Jonas could see. Then he proceeded to identify each value and how it fit into the seven letters of the word.

> **S is for Safety**. The safety of our associates and customers is our highest priority. **E is for Excellence.** Our work is marked by Excellence asking ourselves always, can I put my name on my work today? **R is for Relationship.** We focus on relationship before task. We value people and want to connect and buildi a culture of trusting relationships. **V is for Vision.** Our vision is to serve our customers in an honest, ethical, legal and moral way (H.E.L.M.). **I is for Integrity.** We operate with integrity by the Golden Rule, to treat others like we want them to treat us. **C is Customer.** The customer is at the center of everything that we do. **E is for Empathy**. We want to build solid relationships through connection, communication, and community.

"Wow, I've never worked with anyone who was able to do this so quickly and articulate their core values in such a powerful and simple way!" I guess you do know when you see it, but now you can clearly articulate, cultivate, and teach it to your people. Now it's on to step 2, get feedback from your team and customers. Jonas was genuinely impressed with Jim's written core culture values.

They agreed to meet next week at the same time at the Back Street Café'. Jim was motivated and ready to begin the process of getting feedback and accepting it as it came.

4.

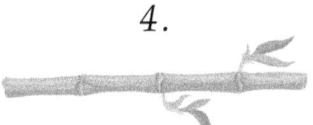

The Feedback

From the time Jim left Jonas at the café' all he could think about was working on his assignment to get feedback from his team, associates and customers. It was time consuming, but he had his assistant block off his schedule so he could focus on this process. She then set-up meetings with the representative groups Jim had targeted.

The first meeting was with his leadership team and then with a cross-section of his broader team, managers, supervisors, and associates. In each of those meetings, before he shared the draft of the culture values and beliefs, he asked, "What do we want to be known for?" After much discussion there were consistently some overall themes that aligned with the values Jim presented.

Then he asked the second question, "What are we known for?"

Jim paused and let that last question settle in before he proceeded with great humility of the current reality.

"To be completely honest we have drifted and it is becoming more and more noticeable. We are drifting as an organization from what we would all agree that we want to be known for. There is definitely a gap between what we want to be known for and how we are known especially to our new bank customer. I take full responsibility for the drift. I have not been a very good example of what we value and I apologize to all of you. With that said, I promise you that I am committed to focus all my effort in getting us back on course and personally be a better leader and example."

"We have always been an organization focused on the customer and putting them in the center of everything we do. Our purpose is to serve and provide services that empower and enhance them. I have drifted in leading you and I believe we have to get back to our root values and beliefs." He then presented a slide with the draft of the culture values and beliefs that make up the acrostic **S.E.R.V.I.C.E.** Jim was eager to allow the team members to question and probe the statements openly and without judgment. He encouraged their honest evaluation and feedback. After working through and tweaking the draft of the values Jim asked, "Does this resonate and sound like what we would like to be known for as a company and how our custormers and community will know us? Are we a company of service with these beliefs and values?"

With every internal group, he went through this same process. Each group was not only affirming, but also excited about the clarity of the beliefs and values that are the very roots of the company's culture. They also helped to provide some clarification and necessary wording changes, but on the whole, they overwhelming affirmed that they are a culture of SERVICE.

Once Jim received feedback internally, he reached out to several customers he has had longstanding, positive relationships with and followed the same process with their key leaders. What humbled Jim more than anything was the incredible feedback he received from his customers about how they had learned so much from his company in the way they treat people. Comments such as:

"We feel like you and your company genuinely care about us."

"We feel like we can trust you and you are trusted advisors."

"We feel like you really can help us and make us succeed and we are better for partnering with you."

"You exemplify service; you lead by serving."

Jim began to reflect and was even more affirmed why they were failing with this new bank client. He realized, *I'm the biggest problem; I'm not living consistently by the beliefs and values that are the roots of who we are as a company. In fact, it has carried over into my personal life as a husband and father. I'm being selfish, self-centered, and playing the victim. I need to get back to the basics! I told Jonas, I knew it when I saw it!* He chuckled to himself.

The next week, at the Backstreet Café', Jim was so eager for his meeting with Jonas and arrived early. In fact, he couldn't sleep the night before and spent time just going over the comments and editing the new culture document. He was excited to get back to Jonas to share the feedback during these sessions and the comments he received that confirmed the WHO and WHY questions that compose the values and beliefs of the company culture.

Jim had the coffee hot and ready for Jonas when he walked through the door. Jonas came in with a big smile on his face and those warm eyes that just draw you in. He was genuinely excited to see everybody he came in contact with, at least that is how it seemed to Jim. Before he got to the booth where Jim was sitting, two different people who greeted him with the hardy handshakes that ended up with a hug stopped him. He was a man that was highly esteemed and loved.

"Jim, I'm sorry that it took me so long to get over here, but those are just such special people and I haven't seen them in such a long time. I do apologize because I value you and your time."

Jim quickly gestured with his hand to sit down and assured Jonas, "No apology needed! You are still 5 minutes early for our meeting. Besides it looks like you are a very popular person around here."

"I appreciate your patience with me. My wife, Sophia, reminds me that I can get a little carried away at times." Thank you for the coffee, as well." He smiled and put his hand on Jim's shoulder as he sat down in the booth.

"I can see by your body language and your facial expression you can't wait to tell me about your week and what you found. So, tell me what happened as you met with the different groups!" Jonas leaned forward, took a sip on his piping hot coffee, and Jim took a deep breath and began sharing.

5.

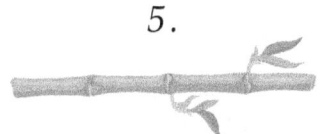

The Bamboo Story

Jim excitedly shared with Jonas how encouraged he was by all the feedback he received about their culture document as well as the input to tweak it in a few places. At this point, Jim was ready to get things started.

"This is great news. The IT of your culture has just been identified and clearly articulated so much so that it resonates with associates and customers. Now comes the hard work over the next 3 to 5 years!" Jonas looked directly into Jim's eyes to watch his reaction to those words.

"What do you mean, 3 to 5 years? You don't understand. This has to work and we have to have results NOW!" Jim's blood pressure was starting to boil and his face turned red. "We don't have that long of time. I'll be lucky if we have 3 to 5 months with this new bank customer if things don't change quickly."

Jonas waited for Jim to calm down and kept looking into his eyes. "Jim, just because you identified WHO you are as a company and WHAT you value doesn't mean that your broader team across diverse demographics is going to get IT overnight. It is a process to cultivate your culture and teach it to people. Just because you have your culture values represented in the acrostic S.E.R.V.I.C.E. doesn't mean people are going to fully align and change immediately."

"But Jonas, 3 to 5 years? I'll be looking for a new job in less than a year if we have to wait that long." Jim's voice sounded defeated and he was starting to exhibit a victim's mentality again.

"Let me ask you. What did you hear me say that triggered this reaction?" Jonas was reminded how this was a familiar pattern that many leaders fall into when they are so focused on the results they misunderstand the priority of PROCESS and PROGRESSION.

"Well, I heard it's going to take 3 to 5 years to be successful." Jim quickly responded.

"Is that what I said or what you heard?" Jonas again looked Jim in the eyes and wanted him to repeat what he had originally said to him.

Jim thought over what Jonas had originally said, "I think you said now comes the hard work over the next 3 to 5 years!"

"That's right, I said NOW the hard work begins over the next 3 to 5 years. I didn't say anything about waiting that long for results. Now begins the hard work of cultivating the culture just like a farmer cultivates a field. It is the hard work of leaders to create an environment where those beliefs and values become part of the PEOPLE who are in your organization. It is going to take at least 3 to 5 years to cultivate and establish those beliefs and values into the thinking, attitudes, behavior, and commitments of your PEOPLE. Even then, like a garden, you have to keep tending and growing it!"

Jim sat up after he heard these words and took another sip of his coffee. "I guess I over reacted. But we still need results right now."

"I certainly understand that you need results now, but your focusing on the wrong priorities to get results now. Let me tell you a story that my Papa, my grandfather, told me that have become the foundation of how I approach leadership and culture. Papa used "The Bamboo Story" to provide an analogy to create a mental framework that challenged and motivated others to reflect on their current reality and to provide a vision for cultivating a change-ready growth culture through servant leadership. The phrase *Remember the Bamboo* is like using a signal word that immediately triggers the brain's understanding of what needs to be the focus of attention individually, at home, in teams, and organizationally as servant leaders.

Jonas continued. "Papa's heart was to transform cultures one person at a time through servant leadership. In his mind, a culture was any environment in which we are placed where we have influence. Thus, at home, work, or play we can habitually, intentionally, and purposely make a difference. He said it was like breathing. As humans, we need oxygen, therefore, we breathe in the oxygen that brings life to our bodies. However, we can breathe out carbon dioxide which, for humans, is life threatening in large quantities. Everyone is breathing, but are we habitually, intentionally, and purposely pumping oxygen or carbon dioxide into our environments. We can choose the air quality of our cultures by the way we think, act, and interact with each other. Speaker, author, and leadership coach, Brian Buffini defines it this way, 'Leadership is a person(s) who creates an environment in which one or more individuals are moved in a coordinated manner toward the accomplishment of a goal.' "

Jim looked more relaxed and Jonas could see he was beginning to change his thinking. "Ok, I am very interested in hearing your Papa's story! Jim exclaimed.

"Great, let me tell you "The Bamboo Story."

The bamboo farmers in Malaysia, using ancient tools and methods that have been passed down through oral tradition for generations, grow a very valuable and profitable strain of bamboo that takes great wisdom and patience to cultivate. In fact, people come from all over the world to find out their secret to such amazing growth and yields. They are often asked questions like this:

Do you have a training program or a manual? The answer is no!

Do you provide training and the immediate response is always yes! You can work with us in the fields and we will show you because you learn by doing.

How long will it take? About 3 to 5 years!

Needless to say they don't get many takers to their training process. What I am about to describe is the bamboo farmer's process and strategy that has been handed down from generation to generation.

During the first year, despite having a multitude of things to attend to, the primary focus of the farmers is on removing the hindrances from the soil that would impede growth. Therefore, they work twelve hours a day to work the soil to remove the impurities and hindrances using the five senses. They feel, study, taste, listen, and smell the soil. When the soil is the perfect consistency, the farmers plant the seed, water, and fertilize. At the end of year one, do you think there was any physical yield?"

Jim immediately responded, "No, how could there be?"

"**During the second year,** the farmers continue to remove the hindrances from the soil, but this year the focus switches

THE BAMBOO STORY

on moisture content. In year two, farmers are working the fields 24/7. Therefore, the precipitation comes either naturally or they irrigate. It must be the perfect consistency. At the end of year two, do you think there was any visible growth or yield?"

Jim again responded, "No!"

"**In year 3,** they go back to the procedure of year 1. Farmers work twelve hours a day with the focus on removing the hindrances from the soil using the five senses At the end of year 3, do you think there is any visible growth or yield?"

Jim just shook his head side to side.

"**In year 4**, the farmers go back to the procedure of year two. The major focus is on the moisture content working the field 24/7. At the end of year 4, do you think there was any visible growth or yield?"

Jim looked a little annoyed at the question this time, but knowing Jonas there was always a lesson he was trying to teach and again he shook his head no.

Year 5 is the year for tremendous growth in just the first 30 days. How much growth do you think would be an outstanding yield for this bamboo crop? Did the crop grow in inches or feet?"

"I don't know, maybe about 6 to 9 feet? I think that would be a good yield." Jim quickly responded.

"Guess again, Jim!"

"Ok, how about 60 feet." He felt he just gave an outrageous number for the growth.

"It is not 9 feet or even 60 feet, but ninety feet in first thirty days of year 5 of the process! The wisdom and patience of the bamboo farmers yields miraculous growth in year 5.

"That is amazing! 90 feet in the first 30 days of year 5!" Jim was genuinely surprised by the amount of growth.

"Jim, what was happening in the first four years that you couldn't see visibly?" Jonas leaned back in the booth and used his hands to point to his eyes.

Jim was in tune with Jonas' question and looked up as he was visualizing and pondering. "I guess there would have to be a huge root system to support 90 foot high bamboo shoots. The roots would have to be almost that deep into the ground."

"Absolutely, in the first 4 years there was tremendous growth in order for the bamboo or fruit to not only survive but to thrive! Growth isn't about the results, but about nurturing the environment or culture so that it is sustainable."

"Now I understand what you were really saying when you stated now the hard work begins and will take 3 to 5 years. It is the cultivating process to grow our company culture's root system deep into who we are and why we exist." Jim smiled and nodded his head as he said the words. He was much more relaxed and calm.

Jonas took the opportunity to ask Jim, "Do you know what the bamboo story can teach us about cultivating a healthy work culture? In fact, do you know how the bamboo story can give you the principles to guide your next steps?"

"Knowing you, I'm sure that you are ready to teach them to me. Seriously, I'm very excited to learn the principles that will move us forward to create a healthy winning culture."

Jonas tore a piece of paper out of his notebook and began to write, starting at the header:

The Bamboo Principles to Grow a Healthy Winning Work Culture

1. *Remove the hindrances to growth*
2. *Cultivating a growth culture takes time and great patience*

3. *The soil (culture) needs a strong and deep root system*
4. *The bamboo farmers (leaders) believe the bamboo will grow and are committed to the process*
5. *Remember that growing bamboo (a change-ready growth culture of servant leaders) will happen progressively through improving the leadership thinking*

"Are you ready to unpack each of these Bamboo Principles?" Jim nodded his head enthusiastically, "Let's get started!"

6.

Remove the Hindrances to Growth

"Jim, the question we now face with your company culture is, **How do we cultivate a new way of thinking and life to make it a healthy, growing, and winning culture?**" Jonas wanted to start with a question to create a reflective dialogue with him over the Bamboo Principles.

Jim was taking notes and reflecting on the question. "I believe that it must begin with the soil, the people, the leadership of the company. Everything rises and falls on leadership. As you have taught me, what are we creating and what are we allowing?"

Jonas smiled and nodded his head. "Absolutely it is about cultivating and growing people. People must be first. Relationship before task. You and your leadership team must live out the values and beliefs of your new culture mantra: SERVICE. You must intentionally and purposely cultivate it and guard it like a gatekeeper. Remember it is more caught than taught.

Jonas paused and made sure that Jim was connecting with what he had just said and saw that he was busy writing down notes. "Using the bamboo farming concept let me share 5 stages in the cultivating process to help remove the hindrances to growth:

REMOVE THE HINDRANCES TO GROWTH

1. We need to first **Remove** the unnecessary debris from the soil, including the weeds, rocks, and anything that would hinder or interfere with the growth of the seed.
2. We **Till** the ground. We break up the soil so that the ground can be receptive to receiving the seeds. This may include adding some new topsoil to aid the process of growth.
3. We **Sow** the seeds. This requires knowledge about the seed and under what conditions that grow best, the right distance from each other, and in the right depth and location.
4. We **Tend** the field. As the bamboo farmers we nurture the garden with the right amount of water and nutrients, and make sure the garden gets the proper amount of sunlight.
5. We must **Guard** the field. Protect the field from insects and other intruders that simply seek to destroy the field for their own self-interests.

Remove, Till, Sow, Tend, and Guard are good active verbs describing the stages of cultivation for a bamboo farmer or a CEO. Jim, how would you translate this into cultivating a work culture?"

Jim looked down at the notes he had just written down and took off his glasses. "It starts with people. We have to have the right people, with the right character, and the right attitude. If not, we have toxic weeds or debris in our soil. I'm, as a leader, responsible for the culture and the environment in the company. It starts with me and what I create and allow in attitudes, behaviors, and mindset of the people who are part of this company. I realize I've allowed the debris in the culture to grow and fester instead of removing and tilling the soil, the people, and the relationships."

Jim stopped, put his glasses back on, and looked down again at his notes. "I have to first sow seeds, which are the right kind attitudes, behaviors, and expectations of this culture. I admit I have not done a very good job of establishing what the values and beliefs are. I need to have courage through the process to be a gatekeeper of what is toxic and make sure that I have the right people, the right processes, the right way of living, and thinking in our culture. If push comes to shove, when the people won't take ownership, when they won't abide by our culture's values, and most of all mindset, then no matter how talented they are, or my loyalty to them in the past, they must be weeded out. Also, my team and me must do better at the hiring process. We have to set-up a process that helps us hire for more than talent and experience, but find people who first and foremost fit our cultural values and beliefs."

As Jim stopped and looked up reflectively, Jonas took the opportunity to affirm what he had just said. "You are seeing very clearly your role and responsibility going forward with cultivating a healthy winning culture. I'm excited for you and the insights that you are gleaning from the bamboo story. Now you are ready as a leader to lead leaders in working in the "bamboo field" of cultural development."

Internally, Jim was sensing and experiencing relief that the cultivation of a winning culture was about how he modeled and intentionally made the culture and values his top priority. It must start with working together with his administrative team. He realized that he was focused on managing the workload instead of leading the work through developing the people.

Jonas continued, "David Rock, author of *Quiet Leadership*,

reminds us of this simple formula: **p = P − I.** Performance (small p) equals our potential (capital P) minus our interference (capital I). People's fears, imagination, self-doubt, self-image, false thinking, etc. get in the way of growth personally and organizationally. Therefore, first and foremost, we must ask, *what are our hindrances or interferences to growth personally and organizationally?* Jim, you and your team now need to live the S.E.R.V.I.C.E. values. As a professor that taught my Papa used to say, 'If you want others to bleed you must be willing to hemorrhage.' Although a little crude, it is a very powerful statement. Everything does rise and fall on leadership and it is more caught than taught."

Let's move to the second principle: Cultivating a positive growth culture takes time and great patience.

7.

The Process is Slow and Fast

"Patience and time is something unfortunately I'm falling short with! Personally, I'm not a very patient person. I like to see things happen right now. Professionally, I don't know if the customer is going to give us the time we need to grow our new culture." As Jim made these statements, Jonas looked into Jim's eyes and could see the fear and anxiety start to mount again.

Sensing this shift in Jim, Jonas shared, "Change is a double-edged sword, on one side change is slow. The literature on change talks about deep transformational change, especially in a work culture, happening in 3-5 and even 5-7 years. However, on the other side of this sword change can be fast. Small changes that reflect **T.R.U.S.T**: Transparency, Respect, Unselfishness, Shared-successes, and Trustworthiness."

"Jim, the more you and your team make yourself **vulnerable** by taking ownership for the issues that are causing you to fail with the bank customer, the more that you see it, own it, solve it, and provide a solution to change, the trust levels can and will be elevated. The real issue now is the customer is asking three questions whether they know it or not: *Does Jim and his company really care about us? Second, can I trust Jim and his team to go forward in a manner consistent with their talk?*

THE PROCESS IS SLOW AND FAST

Third, how can and will Jim and his company provide exactly what they promised going forward? If you can answer those three questions and can operate consistently in walking your talk and talking the walk, trust happens quickly."

Jim took a few seconds to take in what Jonas has just said and reflectively answered, "Then if I understand you correctly the "bamboo process" of growth is both slow and fast. If we take personal accountability and build T.R.U.S.T. with vulnerability and humility by demonstrating that we hear them very clearly. We can show them that we see it and own it and we are committed to solving it with our actions, attitudes, and behaviors."

Jonas quickly affirmed him, "Yes, I believe you've got it on the process of building trust. You see relationships that are open, genuine, respectful, responsible, and most importantly solution-focused that connect deeply on a human level are the foundations of trust."

Jim continued, "Our culture, as we have defined going forward as S.E.R.V.I.C.E is at the heart of who we are, and if we are consistent to act and behave with who we are, we will see the *bamboo* grow." Jim's body language, voice, and face now had the sound of confidence.

"Neuroleadership, also known as brain-based leadership, underscores the mindfulness research through focused sustained attention progressively over time. If we focus our attention, we become or take on the characteristics of what we focus on. If you model and teach this to your company and are the gatekeeper of this on a daily basis, there is no question like the bamboo it will grow. This is not a microwave process, it is more like a crock-pot, and it takes time to cook. However, it starts with you. Remember everything rises and falls with leadership. What you do and how you do it from this day forward is cultivating and planting the seeds that build a strong root system. Leadership is more caught than taught." Jonas was setting the stage to help Jim catch the real heart of leadership.

"What's the difference between a 'good' work culture and a 'phenomenal' business work culture? Jonas looked intently at Jim knowing he was asking a leading question.

Jim looked up and smiled, "I'm not sure, but I bet you're about to tell me."

Jonas chuckled and it broke some of the tension that Jim was feeling. "Turns out there are three things:

1. **Leadership**: Everything rises and falls on leadership and we are never done developing ourselves as leaders, right?
2. **People**: No one succeeds alone. We need a team. Our job as leaders is to attract the very best people and train them well.
3. **Systems**: You can't keep everything in your head and people can't do things 20 different ways, so you need standardized ways to operate that fit your work culture."

Jonas continued, "That's it. Improve your leadership skills to more consistently and progressively lead and model your values and beliefs, hire and/or cultivate great people that fit your culture, install good systems and continuous opportunities for growth and development; and you'll have a better business and a winning culture."

Jim responded, "When you say it like that, it sounds so simple, but I do recognize it is going to be hard work. It sounds like I first have to work on myself, especially in the area of patience. I just had an epiphany of sorts. Isn't this what you really were trying to coach me with for all those months prior to our issue with this new customer?" Jim's tone was emotional as he was realizing that his resistance to personal growth and unwillingness to follow through is at the root of his moving forward.

"Jim, I just want you to know that several years ago I was exactly in the same situation that you are in now. Papa invested his time, life, and legacy into me, but I too was impatient and wanted the microwave version of leadership. It wasn't until I had a crisis of mind and heart did I realize the problem really was me. You are not alone, my friend."

Jonas looked directly into Jim's eyes and said, "Papa told me something that was hard for me to grasp as first. His answer to the question, *what is your greatest challenge as a leader?* It shocked me when I first heard it. He said the greatest challenge, as a leader is to lead yourself! I realized over time the power of those words in my own life. It also brings back some painful lessons I had to learn to grow and develop. I had to be honest with myself that the toughest person to lead is myself. John Maxwell teaches that the first person we must examine is ourselves. He calls it the *Mirror Principle,* which he advises to see ourselves realistically. We have to learn to get out of our own way."

Jonas smiled and continued, "The leaders I know tend to be impatient. They look ahead, think ahead, and want to move ahead. And, of course, that can be good. Being one step ahead makes you a leader, however, it can also be, if you get too far ahead of people, you start looking like the enemy. There is no such thing as instant greatness or maturity as a leader. There are no short cuts, it is a process and it will take root when you are diligent. It takes learning from both successes and failures.

It is all about learning. We need to remember that the point of leadership is not crossing the finish line first. It's about taking people across the finish line with you. Therefore, Jim, we have to slow our pace, stay connected to our people, enlist others to help fulfill the vision, and keep people going. And that my friend takes patience!"

8.

A Strong and Deep Root System

After Jonas finished sharing about patience he stopped and picked up his coffee and asked Jim if he would like another cup. He nodded his head and Jonas walked to the counter to get fresh cups of coffee.

Jim used that time to write down notes and reflect about what he just heard. He thought about his past experiences and this idea that in order to be a successful leader you have to be the strong silent type. A leader that takes it all on yourself and withholds showing emotions, or as he would say it, having a leadership poker face. Jim began to reflect on how he needed to be more vulnerable, open, transparent, and willing to own up to defeats, failures, and shortcomings. He needed to be willing to see it, own it, solve it, and most importantly take positive action. Although, he had a long way to go, he was confident that Jonas would keep him accountable and provide the guidance he needed in this leadership journey.

Jonas placed the cups on table. The smell of the fresh brewed coffee filled the air and paused Jim's realizations.

"Looks like you have been doing some deep thinking and writing," Jonas said as he sat back down in the booth.

"Yes, I have, but I'm really excited to go on to the next bamboo principle. It is all resonating deeply within me."

Both Jonas and Jim took time to bring the hot coffee cups to their lips and blow as they savored the aromatic smell before taking a sip. They nodded in appreciation for the warmth and flavor of the hazelnut coffee.

Jonas looked up and said, "The next principle is the soil or how culture needs a strong root system. **These are the people/leaders who are the foundation of the organization and they need a strong and deep root system in order to thrive.** The core idea here is that culture is something an organization is versus culture as something an organization has. While underground roots are the indispensable foundation of a tree. The bamboo's roots allow it to grow upward and outward and have a solid trunk above ground. Bamboo shoots are known for their solidity. A strong plant does not get destroyed in a storm. It sways, but it stands. The firm roots reflect your solid, unwavering values; your integrity: as you identified and your people have affirmed in your mantra: S.E.R.V.I.C.E."

Jim was nodding his head in agreement and understanding as he took another longer sip of coffee.

"Growth also includes bearing fruit. The deeper the roots, the greater the fruits. In this age of shortcuts and quick fixes, we sometimes forget the principle that roots have to be established downwards before fruit can be borne upward. We all want results and we want them now. We look for shortcuts, hacks, and tips that will get us fame and fortune overnight. But, because the bamboo farmer wants productive plants, he spends more time focusing on watering and fertilizing the soil, so that the roots are thriving and growing more than anything that's happening above ground, even if it takes years to see the results of their labor. As we have already noted, there is always growth. The wisdom of the bamboo farmers is the understanding and priority of growing your people (soil/

culture). It is focusing on the root system, your values, your beliefs, who you are, and why you do what you do first and foremost." Jonas paused as he lifted up his coffee mug and enjoyed another sip.

Jim was taking notes and drew a picture of the bamboo plant and strong root system and labeled the roots with values, beliefs, who you are, and why you do it.

"I'm really understanding my role and top priority as a leader. I need to focus on my people through modeling, teaching, and behaving consistently with our beliefs and values. Cultivating a positive culture of S.E.R.V.I.C.E. means I have to focus my attention on habit development beginning with me. As you always say, *it is more caught than taught.* Then we, myself, and my leadership team, need to intentionally encourage, empower, and equip, those values and beliefs in everything we do. I have to relinquish control of day-to-day operations and business tactics and focus on being a bamboo farmer. I now see it is character driven from the inside out. It must go deep and strong before it grows up tall and wide. But everything rises and falls on my leadership." Jim's face was beaming with a sense of purpose and sense of mission before him.

Jonas smiled and nodded with total affirmation. He knew that Jim was headed to tap into his leadership sweet spot of greatness.

9.

Believe and Commit to the Process

Jonas was taking in all that Jim had just shared and waited for him to finish writing his insights into his notebook before he started on the next bamboo principle.

"Now that we understand the role of a leader is tending to the soil, the people of the culture, the next principle is essential. **Bamboo farmers believe the bamboo will grow and they are committed to the process.** The process of transforming a culture happens one person at a time as their soil is nurtured, cultivated, and hindrances to their growth are removed. Servant leaders must believe and be committed to the process. It is through the process of serving that growth happens because as you just quoted me, *it is more caught than taught.*"

"To create and maintain a thriving organizational culture, each team member must feel valued and passionately believe in the company's values and beliefs. The bamboo farmers are the gatekeepers of the soil, the people. They guard the culture from the impurities that might negatively impact or bring toxicity into the root system. As a leader it is important to remember that your associates and team members represent your company but they also represent your company outside of work. Therefore, it is imperative to hire the right candidates that will represent your company well. In fact, I have created an interview/hiring processes that will help determine if candidates are a culture fit or people who align with the company values."

Jim stopped Jonas and said, "As you were talking about the interview and hiring process. I know that is one of the areas I would love to have you work with us on designing a process that fits our cultural values and beliefs. It is such a laborious and at times costly process. To be honest, it can be very subjective."

"Absolutely, we can help you with the process, but here are some things you can consider when hiring. Start with your culture's values and beliefs and then align your interview and assessment process with them. Every stage of the interview process should have your culture front and center. The culture has to be in the focus of the interview process. The assessment or assessments are needed to give you some more objective data. We can suggest or provide some excellent assessment tools. The assessment should also provide a customized and targeted listed of interview probe questions, and/or coaching questions in relationship to your cultural values and beliefs. The important thing to understand about the assessment process is that it is not a 'personality test' based on anecdotal information.

Jim quickly added, "Part of our challenge on the hiring side of this issue is that we can rarely pick up on character issues through a traditional interview. In my opinion, reviewing a resume and conducting an interview are not enough to ensure that a good hiring decision is being made. Days or weeks later when the new employee is in the job, these character traits become increasingly evident. I definitely know with this huge expansion with the new client, we, and more importantly I have not been successful hiring to fit our culture. I take full ownership because our culture was not clearly defined and it isn't enough to say *I know it when I see it*. I definitely need help with the hiring process as we move forward."

Jonas leaned forward and looked directly into Jim's eyes, "I'm so impressed by your humility and willingness to take full ownership for your culture and your team. Your willingness to take a deep look into the mirror and admit weakness, need, or asking for help is the sign of a true servant leader."

Jim felt deep emotion and a tear formed in the corner of his eye. For the first time in a very long time he felt free to let his emotions show. "Thank you for your encouraging words. They have really resonated deeply within me."

"You are very welcome, and Jim I do believe in you. I know you are in the process of becoming a great servant leader. It reminds me of a book that I have used in teaching and coaching a leadership parable called, *The Secret: What Great Leaders Know and Do* by Ken Blanchard and Mark Miller. I believe it is a classic and it is right in line with the bamboo farmers process, and you will like it because it is an acrostic: S.E.R.V.E."

Jim was writing the word SERVE in his notes, "I love using terms that are easy to remember but resonate deeply with my own heart and passion to lead."

After Jonas went through and taught the SERVE acrostic, Jim was writing vigorously. He sensed an internal switch had been turned on and he had clarity over what he just heard. "Jonas give me a few minutes, I want to share with you the way I summarized what you shared with me from *The Secret* and the SERVE acrostic."

Jim finished writing and looked up with excitement. "Using this content I personalized it to help me communicate and lead my organization." He turned his notebook around so that Jonas could clearly see his notes.

"If I want to lead my organization, I, like the bamboo farmers must believe and commit to the process by focusing on:

S See the future.

I have to clearly communicate a picture of a preferred future, our vision. I have to focus my time and effort each day to communicate not only by my words what we believe and value, but more importantly, by my behavior and actions. I am the guardian of the vision and like water in a bucket, vision evaporates and must be constantly replenished — the vision has to be constantly and repeatedly communicated.

E Engage and Develop Others

I am committed to recruit and select the right people for the right job while creating an environment where people wholeheartedly invest themselves in achieving our vision. My focus is on people and one size doesn't fit all. I will focus my time and energy to help my people grow as a group and individually.

R Reinvent Continuously

I will possess a never-ending focus on improvement. I realize that progress is impossible without change. I will continually ask my team and myself what needs to change in order for us to grow our team, our business, and ourselves. It all must start with me first asking how do I need to change as a leader?

V Value Relationships and Results

I will generate positive, measurable results by cultivating great relationships. Relationship before task mentality. I realize that ultimate success always includes people and performance. My desire each day is: how can I serve you today?

E Embody the Values

More of leadership is caught rather than taught. In other words, people watch the leader and learn from his or her example. I want to live with credibility and live consistently with our stated beliefs and values. I realize if I don't embody the values, the trust of my team and customers will erode, and ultimately I will forfeit the opportunity to lead."

After Jim finished Jonas patted his hand and said enthusiastically, "Jim, you just made what I taught sound so much better because you made it simple but powerful! You put it into your own words and used words like: I will, I want, and I commit. You personalized it and made it your own. You do what great leaders do. You are open to learn and grow because you believe in the process. I'm so proud of you!"

10.

The Leadership Mindset

Jim was struck by Jonas' words to him, *I'm so proud of you!* It struck a deep cord deep within him. It has been a long time since he had heard encouragement and affirmations like the one he had just received. Most of what he experienced was the typical pats on the back for being successful or for doing a good job, but this felt different. Jonas was affirming and encouraging who he is and his innate leadership not his behavior or accomplishments.

"Thank you, Jonas, I appreciate all you are doing for me and bringing out in me."

Jonas smiled, "You are welcome, but all I'm doing is giving you the principles. You are making the applications because they resonate within you."

Jonas took another sip of his coffee, "Are you ready for the last of our bamboo principles?

Jim nodded as he also took another sip of his coffee and immediately picked up his pen to write in his notebook.

"As you know, it is impossible to lead without change, so change is one of a leader's greatest assets. The success and failure of any leader can measured by how one responds to, oversees, and benefits from change. This leads into our last bamboo principle:

Remember that growing bamboo (a change-ready growth culture of servant leaders) will happen progressively through improving the leadership thinking. Again, David Rock, author of *Quiet Leadership*, wrote 'They [organizations] need to instill in their leaders and managers the ability to transform performance by improving their thinking...[they] become compassionate about improving not what people are thinking about, but the way they think.'"

"Jim, when we choose to focus our attention on equipping and empowering people to maximize their leadership potential and attend to a model and process that best allows those values and beliefs of the culture to be cultivated and nurtured, we are building a total context of influence and value where there is consistency between our beliefs, our actions, behaviors, interactions, and relationships."

Jim stopped Jonas at this point and asked, "Are you saying that leadership is all about change?"

"Yes, that is exactly what I'm saying. In both your professional and personal life leadership is ultimately about change. If anyone in a leadership position is passive, disoriented, unresponsive, or overcome by change, this reaction spreads to the whole of the environment around him or her. If there is one thing that leaders must be distinguished by, it is their capacity to respond effectively to change for the sake of those they are leading, as well as for themselves. The leader almost always confronts change first. Therefore, the most important work of leadership is the ability to handle constant confrontation with change. Thus, change is the incubator of leadership thinking."

Jim's face lit up, as he had a moment of insight. "Then my most important work personally or professionally is to focus on my thinking and response to change. Because my response to change affects everyone around me. Then it is my responsibility as a leader to coach and teach others how to embrace a change mentality. I'm beginning to understand one of the main reasons there are negative cultures is because people choose negativity and in reality they have the power to change not only themselves but their cultures."

"Jim again I'm so impressed with your ability to grasp a principle or a concept and clearly articulate it."

Jim smiled, and continued, "So what makes servant leaders different is that they don't focus their attention on the interferences or the difficulty of change, but rather on the mindset and thinking of others. They, to a certain extent, get over themselves and their own 'scar tissue' and focus on others. They are like the bamboo farmers who cultivate their cultures! They influence and add value by their lives through their attitudes, words, and behaviors."

Jim paused and then reflectively said, "My response to the team and bank client was negative, defensive, and lacking true leadership. My thinking was not adding value or positive influence in fact it is the ultimate cause for why we are in the situation we are currently in."

"Again I appreciate your humility and vulnerability. However, that is in the past and now like the bamboo farmers you as a leader are first and foremost a change-agent who thinks, behaves, and acts differently in the midst of difficulties and change. Let me share five ways people typically approach change. Understanding the five approaches will help you to tend to your mindset and the mindset of others.

Approach #1: We just watch things happen. This is a passive, indifferent approach to change. Leaders don't react to change because they have no real interest or awareness of its impact.

Approach #2: We just let things happen. This is a resigned, defeated, or victim's mentality to change. You can complain or even lash out to change, but ultimately our mindset is, there *is nothing I can do about this.*

Approach #3: We ask, what happened? This is an inquisitive approach, but it doesn't go much further than mere curiosity or interest in the latest gossip surrounding the change. It can also mean that you never saw the change coming and therefore were not prepared to respond to it.

Approach #4: We defy what happens. This is when someone tries to resist the inevitable change in his or her life, wasting valuable time and energy in the process. We rehash, ruminate, and complain about the change. However, the only result is your own stress and internal frustration increases.

Approach #5: We make things happen. This is a proactive approach that either alters the quality or degrees of change that happens or that initiates new change. This is a growth mindset mentality that sees it, owns it, solves it, and takes action. When you have this approach and mindset you are usually the ones who succeed in life — against all odds. They have grit and preserve under difficulties, pressure, and of course change."

"Jonas, I can see now that especially in my dealing with the new bank customer and my team, my thinking approach had a bit of each of the first four approaches, especially number four. I've spent so much wasted time defying the process of change in our culture and with the client. I'm really guilty of the victim's mentality."

"Jim it is so easy for our thinking and mindset to go to the negative that is our automatic response. That is why, as a leader, it is so important to master your thinking or your thinking will master you. Like the bamboo farmers it is constantly weeding the field to get rid of the interferences to growth. They teach to focus our attention on what is most important and how to see extraordinary growth become possible.

We can either be our own worst enemy or our own greatest ally. Our perspective is being shaped by our internal belief system, and our internal belief system will either take on a victim's mentality or victor's mentality. When we take approach number five, we are embracing change as being inevitable and working through the process with a positive growth mindset."

Jim nodded in acknowledgement and thoughtfully asked, "How can I be more proactive and intentional in creating an environment that improves leadership thinking?"

"That is a great question and let me try to give you a simple idea that has emerged from psychology, cognitive science, linguistics, neuroscience, and rooted in ancient wisdom. Allan Deutschman wrote an excellent book based on this research called, Change *or Die: Could You Change When Change Matters Most?* I love this title and of course the content, but the process of change can be very threatening, so it helps if we learn new skills, and mindset through relationships." Jonas looked through his notebook and found a one-page document entitled Change or Die: Keys to Transformational Change.

"I'm so glad I had this document I created a few years ago in my notebook. I believe this will answer your questions about creating an environment that improves leadership thinking." Jonas positioned the page so that Jim could see it as he talked through each of the points. He pointed at the first point,

"The First Key to Transformational Change to Improve Leadership Thinking is to **RELATE**. Form a new, emotional relationship with a person or culture that inspires and sustains hope. People need a leader or leaders who restore your hope—to make you believe you can change. The leaders and/or culture have to sell you on yourself and make you believe you have the ability to change. They have to sell you on themselves as your partners, mentors, role models, or sources of new knowledge. And they have to sell or persuade you on the specific methods or strategies that they employ."

"Jonas, you are a perfect example of this first key point. You have inspired me by your encouragement, belief in me, and positive optimism. You have created a hopeful reality that we will see transformational change happen and I have what it takes to see it happen."

"Thank you for your kind words. I do believe in you and I know you can lead the process of transformational change one person at a time. That perfectly leads us into the Second Key to Transformational Change to Improve Leadership Thinking, which is to **REPEAT.** The new relationship and/or culture helps you learn, practice, and master the new habits and skills that you'll need. So as I said before, here is where the hard work begins over the next three to five years. Just as I will coach and mentor you, you in turn must coach and mentor your team. It takes a lot of repetition over time before new patterns of thinking and behavior become automatic and seem natural—until you act the new way without even thinking about it. Papa was my teacher, coach, and mentor who gave me guidance, encouragement, and direction along the way. Transformational change doesn't involve just "selling;" it requires training.

The Third Key to Transformational Change to Improve Leadership Thinking is to **REFRAME.** The new relationship and/or culture help you learn new ways of thinking about your situation and your life. Ultimately, you look at the work in a way that would have been so foreign to you that it wouldn't have made any sense before you changed. When you reframe your thinking you are in the constant process of progressive growth and development. You have a growth mindset that sees obstacles and difficulties as opportunities to see it, solve it, own it, and do it. It becomes a culture of accountability and extreme ownership. We see leaders and a culture that becomes solution focused and not problem focused. Individuals who don't act like employees, but instead act like they are owners of the business."

Jim finished writing down the last key point and shrugged his shoulders and shook his head. "I have to admit these three keys to transformational change sound simple; almost too good to be true."

"This may sound simple at first, but let me assure you, it's not. Change of any kind is about learning new habits and skills that inform new ways of thinking. Change is all about training and teaching, but it takes a lot of "selling" to motivate people to sustain the necessary effort over time. Most people and organizations still embrace a false view of the change process and employ traditional methods that I describe as the **3Fs: Facts, Fear, and Force.** We just need to give people the facts or more information and then they will change. Facts and information may get a person thinking, but it doesn't teach them new habits or skills to change. The idea of just scaring them with ads or pictures that shows the consequence of not changing. This will work temporarily but it will not be sustainable overtime. The weight loss industry is the perfect example of this. Fear can also be used to force people to change. Again, that might work temporality, but it is not sustainable over time. People spend billions of dollars every year buying self-help books, webinars, videos, joining health clubs, diet programs, seeing doctors, therapists, hiring life coaches, and business consultants and yet so often they fail to realize their goals. The reason isn't that they don't want to change or can't change, but rather they don't understand change or have the right tools to make it happen. We have embraced a false view of the change process, especially our reliance on facts and fear. The best research about change in companies and organizations has been led by John Kotter, a professor at Harvard Business School, who concluded that changing organizations depends overwhelming on changing the emotions of their individual members which underscores the 3Rs of Relate, Repeat, and Reframe. When it comes to transformational change it is less a matter of giving people more information or analysis to influence their thoughts than helping them to see a truth to influence their feelings. Both thinking and feeling are essential, and both are found in thriving healthy cultures, but the heart of change is in emotional connection we make with people or a culture that inspires hope."

As Jonas was talking him through the keys to transformational change, Jim reflected on how important relationships and people are over the task or the work. He came to grips with how much time he had wasted trying to "fix" the situation with the bank client instead of just leading the change process. "Jonas I will never forget this time we have spent together and how much you have inspired and taught me. I now have a hopeful reality. I look forward to working together with you to grow the bamboo. It's time to start cultivating this S.E.R.V.I.C.E. culture. I know that I will always remember the bamboo!"

11.

The Process of Developing a Healthy Culture

Jim and his leadership team were excited to meet with Dr. Jonas Nolan to work on the process of developing a healthy culture. There was a sense of excitement in the air. Three days were set-aside in their calendars to work with Jonas and develop a strategic approach to cultivating and teaching the culture. Dr. Nolan and his team designed and facilitated a highly interactive and appropriately challenging agenda for the training sessions.

Jonas began the sessions on the first morning with *Developing a Healthy Culture Model* overview. "As you know, we are in the process of cultivating the bamboo!" Members of the team chuckled as they were by now all familiar with the bamboo story.

"Our task is to clearly *define, teach, practice, measure and model* this culture in how we behave, interact, and treat others." Remember that culture represents how works get done, from how you make decisions, to how you run meetings, to how you assign projects, to how you reward effort, to how you hire, to how you develop your associates." He turned on the projector and the following model was presented to the leadership team.

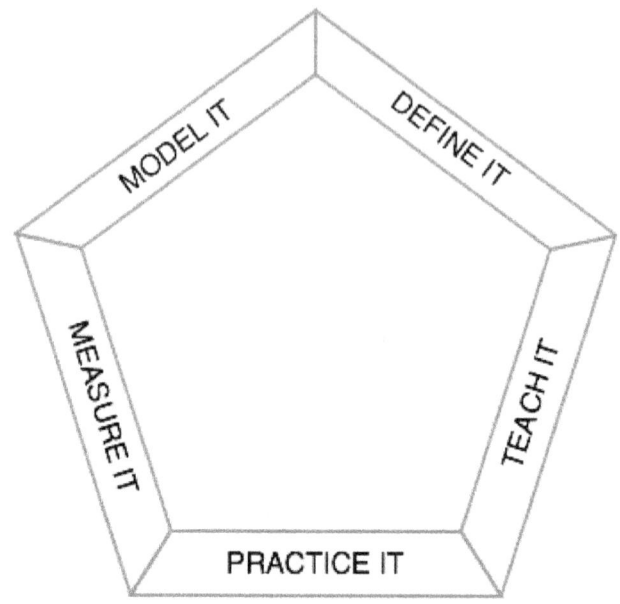

"Let me take you through each step of this model. **Step 1: Define IT.** I like this quote from John Maxwell, *'A company's culture is the expression of the values of the people, not a reflection of what you want it to be. People do what people see — and they keep doing it. What people do on an ongoing basis creates culture.'* First and foremost culture is an expression of the values of the people within the organization not a reflection of what you want it to be.

He clicked on to the next slide:

"You as a team under Jim's leadership have clearly defined a working definition of what this business values and how you will conduct business. You spent time testing and getting feedback around your core values of **S.E.R.V.I.C.E..** "**S is for Safety**. The safety of our associates and customers is our highest priority. **E is for Excellence.** Our work is marked by Excellence asking ourselves always can I put my name on my work today? **R is for Relationship.** We focus on relationship before task. We value people and want to connect and buildi a culture of trusting relationships. **V is for Vision.** Our vision is to serve our customers in an honest, ethical, legal and moral way (H.E.L.M.). **I is for Integrity.** We operate with integrity by the 'Golden Rule' to treat others like we want them to treat us. **C** is for Customer. The customer is at the center of everything that we do. **E is for Empathy.** We want to build solid relationships through connection, communication and community. So step 1 is completed and extremely clear."

"**Step 2 is Teach IT**: This is where we as team need to focus our attention and time for the bulk of our training sessions together beginning right after I complete this overview process. This is the heart, head, and hands of how we ensure that everyone in our organization knows our leadership and cultural point of view and leaders at all levels have the skills required to succeed in it."

"**Step 3 is Practice IT:** In this step we have to put this training into action and create opportunities for leaders and emerging leaders to lead! We must provide an environment where we give them stretch assignments to prove and improve them as leaders. A safe environment where they are mentored and coached with a balance of caring and candor. It's when encouragement and constructive feedback are offered so that they can grow both personally and professionally.

"**Step 4 is Measure IT**: we have to assess our leadership development efforts adjusting strategies and tactics accordingly. We have to establish both qualitative and quantitative measures and key performance indicators. You can't score a goal if you can't see the goal line. At this step, we want to talk in terms of results. People can confuse work with results, particularly when it comes to personal and leadership growth. Clearly define desired outcomes by specifically workstating what 'rings the bell.' A key performance indicator could be: We make the customer the center of what we do, by focusing our actions and interactions on what they need and making them feel valued over 95% of the time. For example, create a monthly customer satisfaction survey that asks questions directly related to your cultural values. Like on a scale of 1 to 5, five meaning definitely and 1 meaning never: *Would you hire the member of the team you interact with the most? Did the member of team or our organization make you feel valued and a priority?'* Ask your team, to talk about success stories that they have heard or been a part and make a regular part of your team meetings. My team and I have a rich background in the measurement area and will work with you if you need help to customize the assessment process for your organization."

"**Step 5 is Modeling IT**, we have to **walk the talk and talk the walk.** We have to lead by example because everything rises and falls on leadership. Starting with Jim and everyone here who is part of this leadership team, we have to live the culture out in our daily actions and routines. Again, as Dr. Howard Hendrick's once said: *If you want others to bleed you must be willing to hemorrhage.* A crude illustration, but it hammers home an important point. The success or failure of this culture is in the hands of its leaders. It is how you think, your attitude in any given situation, how you behave, and how consistent you are with the message you are delivering. People are really looking for at least three things from their leaders: **character, consistency, and connection."**

Jonas looked around the room making eye contact with each and every leader as he passionately emphasized their role and mission and making this a winning and successful culture. Inspired, they met his eyes motivated and determined to live up to being purpose-driven leaders. "Now that you have an overview of the steps, are you ready to get to the hard work of strategically working on how to teach and implement this?"

Over the next two days Jim and his leadership aided by Jonas and his team went to work on developing a systemic approach to cultivating and teaching the heart, head, and hands of their culture. With the guidance of Jonas, the team realized that virtually all training takes care of the information part of the equation. And that is good. People need information. However, in order to thrive and be successful, the training must go beyond information and address the motivation of the learner and help them to grow both personally and professionally.

"Most organizations are focused on 100% information in the training process. We assume that the learners will be motivated. But remember, change is hard. Motivation matters. Because change is hard, we need to make change easier—not easy, but easier. We must find ways to support the learning process and apply it to the real world. Our desire is that long after the training the learners will be transformed from the inside out. This can take on many forms: coaching, accountability, resources, communities of practice, and so on. In fact, to be perfectly honest the training sessions are only about 10% of the transformation process. It is more about assessment of their current reality of thinking and living, principles and skills that can be easily understood and applied, and then relevancy into their current situation and life circumstances at work and at home. Our challenge going forward is to do all we can to improve the information—but also to find ways to help with the motivation and certainly connection to people and their situations."

Jonas paused and looked at each member of Jim's team and then said, "As I mentioned before, the success and failure of this transformation is your level of involvement, support, and most importantly your modeling the culture and its values. Remember the culture and values are **more caught than taught!** It is relational connection, clarity of communication, and authentic leadership."

At the end of the sessions the team had developed comprehensive plans: one for the a pilot program to begin with Jim's leadership team and some other key leaders and another for a system wide introduction of the *why, what and how* of cultivating a healthy winning culture. Each of the interactive and reflective training modules focused on the individual and team's thinking, actions, and interaction that nurture and model the organizations cultural values. Giving leaders and team members the tools and strategies that would empower them to effectively lead and serve their teams and customers more effectively.

Jim met with Jonas and reviewed the plans. They were in agreement that Jonas and his team would facilitate and teach the process in person workshops or via webinars. At the end of the meeting, Jim knew the organization was about to take a giant leap forward. He was grateful that his team was taking the necessary steps to make it to the next level. He thought to himself, "We aren't a thriving bamboo culture yet, but I have hope and I'm very optimistic.

He turned looking deeply into Jonas' eyes, smiled and said, "Jonas, I'm so grateful I'm on this journey with you and I know that the bamboo will grow!"

12.

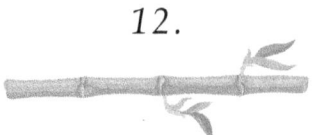

The Bamboo is Growing

In the days and months that followed, Jim reflected on all the things he'd learned during his meetings with Jonas. He realized that his time with him had made a profound impact on him. It had certainly changed his leadership focus and mindset. He would never look at leadership, his team, or culture in the same way again.

As he was applying the principles from the bamboo story, he felt a new energy and enthusiasm that truly amazed him. The performance of his team and business group continued to improve. The goals they set around their culture values and beliefs of S.E.R.I.V.C.E. were very aggressive, yet everyone on his team felt they were achievable. They all now believed that they could win the bank client over. They decided the key would begin first with serving their client with unprecedented levels of customer service and second, working together as a team to live out their culture values and beliefs. The system wide training process had been implemented throughout his organization.

Jim was deep in thought and preparing his heart and mind for the meeting with the new bank client's CEO, Cheryl Chatwood and her team. "All of these transformational changes are the result of my conversations with Jonas Nolan.

He pushed me to become a different kind of leader, and that has made all the difference. He is the key relationship that has inspired hope and belief that I can lead and reframe my thinking and the thinking of all whom I influence. I guess it is true, everything does rise and fall on leadership."

The alarm on his phone went off and it startled him. It was time to get to the meeting. As he walked down the hallway from his office to the conference room, he encountered Paula, his Vice President of Operations. "Before we go into this meeting, I want to thank you for all the help you've given me over the past few months. Our 1:1 meetings have really got me thinking. You listen and ask me interesting and very thought-provoking questions. They have challenged me to examine my life and especially how I interact with people both at work and at home. Thank you for teaching and coaching me. But most of all, thank you for listening to me and hearing me so that you could ask me just the right question at the right time. I've learned so much from you about focusing on relationship before the task."

Jim was caught off guard; Paula was a quiet, analytical person. She held what she was feeling and thinking close to the vest. She could have been an excellent poker player because she was often very difficult to read. This was the first time that she expressed gratitude to Jim in such an open and vulnerable way.

"Thank you for your kind words that means so much to me. It really is the encouragement that I needed walking into this meeting with the bank client." Jim warmly smiled at Paula and touched his hand to his heart to show how much he appreciated her comments as they walked through the conference door together.

The conference room had been prepared for the meeting

and all the materials and technology were ready to go. The bank officials and members of Jim's team were huddled around a table in the back of the conference room filled with breakfast pastries, fruit, coffee, and juices. This was the fourth quarter business review. The bank's CEO, Cheryl, the CFO, COO, and three of their top Senior Vice Presidents representing all of the regions across the nation were enjoying small talk, sipping coffee, and munching on the breakfast goodies. Jim was confident, but just like any big meeting or athletic contest he participated in, he was feeling the 'pre-game jitters' and butterflies in his stomach.

After some personal greetings and handshakes, Jim's assistant, Pam, made the announcement to start moving to their seats at the conference table. Jim began the meeting with a very personal and heartfelt introduction of each member of the client's team and then a thank you to his team. He focused his gratitude on the members who were responsible for organizing and getting all of the details of the meeting together. "Without Pam and her team none of this would be possible. They are the glue that holds us all together and makes sure we have exactly what we need to be successful, and of course the best breakfast spread."

Around the room there was a collective chuckle and nod of approval about breakfast. Jim then began his presentation, "Over the past year, I've learned some great lessons, but none greater than this; as a leader I can't blame or point the finger at others, I must own my actions and outcomes. At the beginning of this past year, I was failing you, my bank clients, and my team members. My mentor and coach, Dr. Jonas Nolan, reminded me that everything rises and falls on leadership. I was not doing a very good job of leading and/or serving all of you.

As you know, over the past year we have made changes, transformational changes to better serve the bank and all of our customers in a very intentional purposeful way. We strive to bring all of our clients extraordinary service and to consistently live out our values and beliefs in our behaviors and actions. We have made progress, but we have room to grow and develop in the process. We are not perfect but we are progressing and getting better each and every day. I must admit, I can be a better leader and have room to grow."

Jim clicked on the projector to the slide presentation and the first slide was their **S.E.R.V.I.C.E.** culture statement and values with colorful graphics and animations. Then he proceeded to identify each value and how it fit into the seven letters of the word.

There was a look of surprise especially from Cheryl. She wasn't surprised by what Jim said, but she was surprised that he didn't start the meeting off in the traditional way with financials, cost savings, try to schmooze her with how well things were going and all that they were doing for the bank. She was challenged by Jim's approach and most of all his humility. She had observed Jim over this past year and had seen the radical change in him and how his company truly was consistently and positively responding to them even when they were unreasonable, impatient, and frankly down right rude.

Then, Jim said this, "Over this past year, we are continually asking ourselves: *'how are we doing the work? How can we do it better? What changes would enhance our ability to serve our customers and each other?* These are the questions that are constantly on my mind and the team's mind to better serve you, our customer. What I have realized and want to continue to understand is that we can get even better financial results if we have good relationships. We have to raise the value of our relationship to be better listeners and in turn better communicators. We have traditionally focused on teaching our people important skills they need to get results: problem solving, decision-making, and so on. However, what I have to continue to work on myself and then teach is building relationships and connecting with people to help them continually to perform better. What my team and I continue to discover is when we place emphasis on relationships we listen to people, invest time with them, care deeply about them, and are recognizing their efforts."

Cheryl thought to herself, "Jim's message is resonating with me. Here is a leader who is open, honest, transparent, and extremely vulnerable. He is admitting he doesn't have it all figured out. Boy, is this rare! It is so refreshing to hear and experience. The corporate world is anything but humble and I know I can learn from Jim's example."

After Jim finished his presentation, he was about to ask for questions before he turned the rest of the presentation over to his team. Cheryl interrupted, "Jim I want you to know that not only do I believe what you just presented, but there really is no need to proceed."

There was a hush silence in the room, it was like all of the air just got sucked out of the room and time froze. It seemed like an eternity, but it was just a matter of seconds that ticked by before Cheryl smiled and added, "I've heard enough to know that you and your company are our trusted partners moving forward. You all have worked so hard over the course of this past year that I want you to know that we are awarding you with an extended contract that will cover all of our expansion over the next 5 years!"

Jim's mouth dropped wide open and the biggest smile

THE BAMBOO IS GROWING

even bigger than Jonas Nolan's radiated from him. "I don't know what to say, but thank you is not enough."

"Jim, you and your team have earned our trust after that very shaky start. We certainly want to hear the rest of your team's presentation, but I just had to tell you up front where we stand with you going forward. In fact, there is so much I believe we can learn from you and your culture. We are really interested in partnering together and learning from one another. One of your team members was telling a few of us about the bamboo principles."

All Jim could see was the image of Jonas Nolan smiling that smile at him when told him I see greatest in you and I believe in you. A small tear formed in his right eye and he said to Cheryl. "Of course, if you don't mind, let me tell you the bamboo story."

Epilogue

What's the most valuable asset to your organization? It's the people, hands down, which is why it's so important to have a healthy culture. So what is culture? In simple terms, culture is the way **people think, act, and interact.** Culture is all about the people. Culture is influenced and shaped by the messages verbally and nonverbally they receive from their leader(s).

You have followed Jim Thor's inner struggle and tensions and observed his working through his personal and professional leadership battle with the caring guidance and influence of his executive leadership coach Dr. Jonas Nolan. Now ask yourself, as he did, *"What is my deepest fear? What is holding me back from my sweet spot of leadership greatness?"* Leadership is influence and no matter if you are a CEO, a stay at home dad or mom, a trades person, a laborer, student, a parent, etc., we all have influence and influence creates and impacts culture.

Jonas shared with Jim the principles of building a healthy and winning culture through the lessons he learned from his Papa: "The Bamboo Story Principles." Much like the bamboo, the culture is the process of growing the way *people think, act, and interact.* It is a process and the first and foremost priority of leadership is the development his or her people. How do you grow an organization? You grow the people and to grow others you first must grow yourself.

Just like a family, if the parents' relationship is dysfunctional, the family will be too. That's not to say that some good things can't come out of it; it's just the family/organization will not come anywhere close to realizing its full potential. John Maxwell says. "Everything rises and falls with leadership." The health of an organization's culture is its greatest advantage.

Like Jim, are you are at a point in your life where your deepest fear is being exposed and brought to light? Is it time for you to unleash the true leader in you? Is it is time for you to journey into your destiny and assignment that only you were born to accomplish? Is it time to breakthrough the barriers that are holding back your leadership influence?

Are you ready, like Jim, to draw from the wisdom of the Bamboo Story? Transforming cultures begins one person at a time. Are you willing to step into your leadership sweet spot of greatness?

References

Autry, J., (2001). *The Servant Leader*, Three Rivers Press, New York, NY.

Blanchard, K. & Miller, M.(2004, 2009, 2014). *The Secret: What Great Leader Know and DoBerrett-Koehler Publishers*, Oakland, CA.

Collins, J. (2001). *Good to Great*, Harper Business, New York, NY.

Covey, S. (1991). *Principle Centered Leadership*, Random House, New York, NY.

Covey, S.(1989). *The Seven Habits of Highly Effective People*, Simon and Schuster, New York, NY.

Covey, S. (2004). *The 8th Habit: From Effectiveness to Greatness*, Simon and Schuster, New York, NY.

Covey, S.M.R. (2006). *The Speed of Trust: The One thing that Changes Everything*, Simon and Schuster, New York, NY.

De Pree, M. (1997). *Leading without Power*, Jossey-Bass, San Francisco, CA.

De Pree, M. (1988). *Leadership is an Art*, Double Day, New York, NY.

Deutschman, A. (2007). *Change or Die: Could You Change When Change Matters,* Harper-Collins, New York, NY.

Edmondson, A. (2008, July-August). The competitive imperative of learning. Harvard Business Review. 60-67.

Glaser, J. E., (2006). *The DNA of Leadership: Leverage Your Instincts to Communicate, Differentiate, Innovate,* Platinum Press, Avon, MA.

Goleman, D. & Boyatzis, R. (2008, September). Social Intelligence and the Biology of Leadership. Harvard Business Review. 74-81.

Greenleaf, R. K., (1983) *Servant Leadership.* Paulist Press, New York, NY.

Hassed, C. (2008) Mindfulness, wellbeing and performance. NeuroLeadership Journal [1} 53-60.

Irving, J.A., & Longbotham, G.J. (2007). Team effectiveness and Six Essential Servant Leadership Themes: A regression model based on items in the Organizational Leadership Assessment. International Journal of Leadership Studies [2] 2. 98-113.

Jensen, R. (2001) Achieving *Authentic Success,* Life Coach Foundation, San Diego. CA.

Jung-Beeman, M, Collier, A. & Kounios, J. (2008). How insight happens: learning from the brain. NeuroLeadership Journal [1] 20-25.

Kotter, J. (1996). *Leading Change*, HBS Press, Boston, MA.

Kotter, J.(1999). *What Leaders Really Do*, HBS Press, Boston, MA.

Kotter, John (2002) *The Heart of Change*, HBS Press, Boston, MA.

Kriegel, R. & Brandt, D. (1996). *Sacred Cows Make the Best Burgers: Developing Change Ready People and Organizations*, Warner Books, New York, NY.

Lencioni, P., (2002). *The Five Dysfunctions of a Team*, Jossey-Bass, San Francisco, CA.

Lencioni, P., (2012). *The Advantage: Why Organizational Health Trumps Everthing Else in Business*, Jossey-Bass, San Francisco, CA.

Liberman, M. & Eisenberger, N. (2008). The pains and pleasures of social life: a social cognitive neuroscience approach. NeuroLeadership Journal [1] 38-43.

Ochsner, K. (2008). Staying cool under pressure: insights from social cognitive neuroscience and their implications for self and society. NeuroLeadership Journal [1] 26-32.

Maxwell, J. 1993). *Developing the Leader Within You*, Thomas Nelson, Nashville, TN.

Maxwell, J. (1999). *Failing Forward*, Thomas Nelson, Nashville, TN.

Maxwell, J. (2000). 21 Irrefutable Laws of Leadership, Thomas Nelson, Nashville, TN.

Maxwell, J. (2003). *Think For A Change*, Warner Business Books.

Monroe, M. (2009). *Becoming a Leader: Discovering the Leader you were meant to be!*, Whitaker House, New Kensington, PA.

Monroe, M. (2008). *In Charge: Finding the Leader within You*, FaithWords, New York, NY.

Monroe, M. (2005). *The Spirit of Leadership: Cultivating the attitudes that influence human action*, Whitaker House, New Kensington, PA.

Rath, T. & Clifton, D. (2004). *How Full is Your Bucket?* Gallup Press, New York, NY.

Rock, D. (2008). SCARF: A brain-based model for collaborating with and influencing others. NeuroLeadership Journal [1] 44-52.

Rock, D. (2006). *Quiet Leadership: Six Steps to transforming performance at work*, Harper-Collins, New York, NY.

Rock, D., & Schwartz, M. (2006). The Neuroscience of Leadership. Breakthroughs in brain research explain how to make organizational transformation succeed. Strategy + Business. www.strategy-business.com/article/062007.

Schwartz, J., & Begley S. (2002). *The Mind and the Brain: Neuroplasticity and the Power of Mental Force.* Harper-Collins, New York, NY.

Senge, P, (1999). *The Dance of Change: The Challenges of Sustaining Momentum In Learning Organizations,* New York, NY Doubleday-Currency.

Senge, Peter (1990). *The Fifth Discipline: The Art and Practice of the Learning Organization,* New York, NY Doubleday-Currency.

Stabile, M. (2013). *Papa's Legacy: A Leadership Parable,* FutureNow Consulting, Naples, FL.

Stabile, M. (2016). *The Heart, Head, and Hands of a Servant Leader: Unleashing Personal Greatness to Serve Others,* FutureNow Consulting, Naples, FL.

Stabile, M. (2019). *Unlocking Buried Treasure: Keys to Mastering Your Greatest Fears,* Outskirts Press, Parker, CO.

About The Author

Michael J. Stabile, Ph.D. uses his extensive leadership training in a wide variety of vocations: education, leadership and life coaching, consulting, and writing. But the same theme permeates his many positions of influence: he is passionate about inspiring and empowering others to be change agents in their homes, jobs, and communities.

Mike's company, *FutureNow Consulting LLC*, uses workshops, seminars, and customized life coaching to affect transformational change at the individual, group, and organizational levels.

Mike and his wife, Pam, live in Naples, Florida They are blessed with three married daughters and seven grandchildren.

If you are interested in contacting Mike for workshops, keynote speaking, or a presentation based on concepts presented in this book, contact him at mstabile@futurenowed.com *or visit his website for additional workshop information or services of FutureNow Consulting, LLC at* www.futurenowed.com.

This book is part of the **Leadership Parable Series.** The author calls these "sticky stories," which help the reader to remember the key lessons from the parables, and is intended to create a mental framework about the influence of a servant leader. **Mike's books available through Amazon and other major book retailers.**

Also part of the Leadership Parable Series: *Papa's Legacy*

The underlying truth lesson: "to serve is to lead" is portrayed through the heart-felt relationship between a man and his Papa (grandfather.) This simple story provides an emotional connection and backdrop to help the reader reflect on how servant leadership is more "caught than taught." Therefore, this story creates a mental framework that can challenge and motivate you, the reader, to reflect on your current reality, providing the motivation and inspiration to cultivate your own "garden of influence." Our world is suffering from a lack of leadership, but you can help make a difference. Whether you know it or not, you have the ability within you to lead by serving. Cumulatively, we can create an army of servant leaders, leaving behind a leadership legacy for future generations. Will you be part of Papa's legacy?

Also part of the Leadership Parable Series: *Unlocking Buried Treasure: Keys to Mastering Your Greatest Fears*

What is my deepest fear? In every sense of the word, Nicole is successful. She has a thriving career, a loving husband, and beautiful children. For Nicole, though, a constant voice in the back of her mind tells her that all these things are not good enough, that she is not good enough. In this leadership parable, follow Nicole's inner conflict and struggles as she meets with the two people she trusts the most, Dr. Jonas Nolan and his wife, Sophia. With the loving guidance and coaching by the Nolans, ask yourself as Nicole did, "What is my deepest fear? What is holding me back from my sweet spot of greatness?" Like Nicole, are you are at a point in your life where your deepest fear is now being exposed and brought to light? Is it time for you to unlock the buried treasure within you? Is it time for you to journey into your destiny and assignment that only you were born to accomplish? Is it time to be liberated from fear? Unlocking Buried Treasure: Keys to Master Your Greatest Fear not only shows how to identify the fears that are holding you back but also gives you accessible and tangible strategies and keys to overcome those fears so you can reach your greatest potential, both personally and professionally.

Also by Michael J. Stabile the Book and Workbook: *The Heart, Head, and Hands of a Servant Leaders: Unleashing Personal Greatness to Serve Others*

Whether you're an account executive or a stay-at-home mom, you can effect transformational change if you learn to access the spirit of leadership imprinted on your DNA.

In a world of innumerable books and workshops on leadership, life coach Michael J. Stabile, PhD, provides the "missing link" between the desire to lead and the ability to lead well: following Jesus's example by learning that all leaders, great and small, are servants.

Stabile breaks down the fundamentals of servant leadership into three parts:

- Why are your "heart," "head," and "hands" so important? In Part 1, explore Stabile's unique claim that servant leadership is hardwired into your genetic coding and is critical for success.
- What are a leader's heart, head, and hands? In Part 2, find that "sweet spot" of leadership greatness by attaching your gifts to God's purposes.
- How do you integrate your heart, head, and hands to maximize leadership potential? In Part 3, acquire practical tips and tools backed by science and biblical truth.

This companion workbook is designed to further your thinking and reflection on what it means to be a servant leader in all parts of your life. It is a powerful tool for individuals, teams, and organizations. This workbook asks you to take the time to reflect, brainstorm and create an action plan to create lasting and transformational change on your journey to becoming a servant leader. Using the concepts from the book, the workbook creates an avenue to interact and put into action the ideas and recommendations to create lasting change in you both personally and professionally. This is an excellent resource to use for deeper self-study, an accountability group or a partnership to go through the workbook together.

www.ingramcontent.com/pod-product-compliance
Lightning Source LLC
Chambersburg PA
CBHW070315230526
45470CB00002B/882